What is Montessori?

Written and Photographed by Kelly Ekue

Montessori is
a science,
a method,
an art.

Grace and courtesy are taught from the start.

The senses are used;
they connect
with the mind.

Purposeful work, neatly displayed you will find.

The environment is aesthetic and carefully prepared, for the child to discover and become more aware.

There are materials that show our place in the world.

From the concrete to abstract, talents are unfurled.

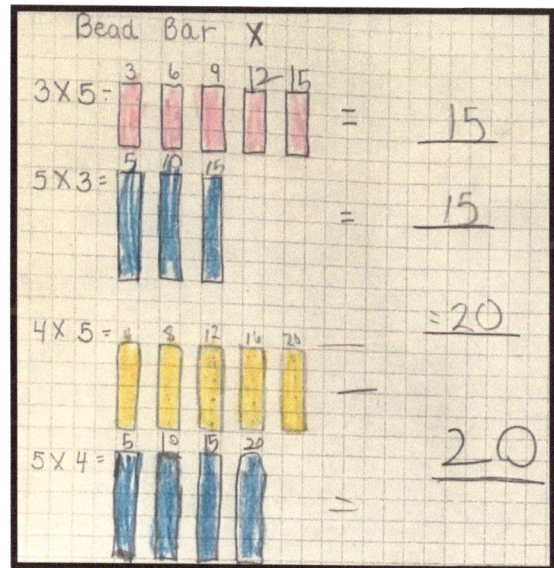

With a tower and stairs, three-part cards and beads,

Montessori seeks what the child needs.

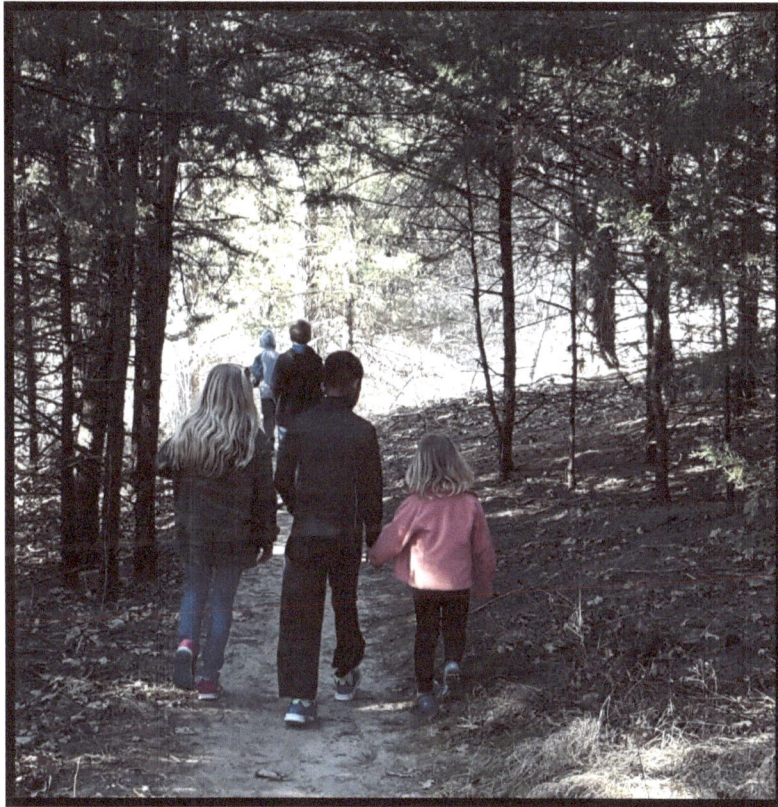

On the path to learn, the teacher serves as a guide.

There are
lessons of peace.

We feel calm inside.

We are part of the cosmos and we learn the theories.

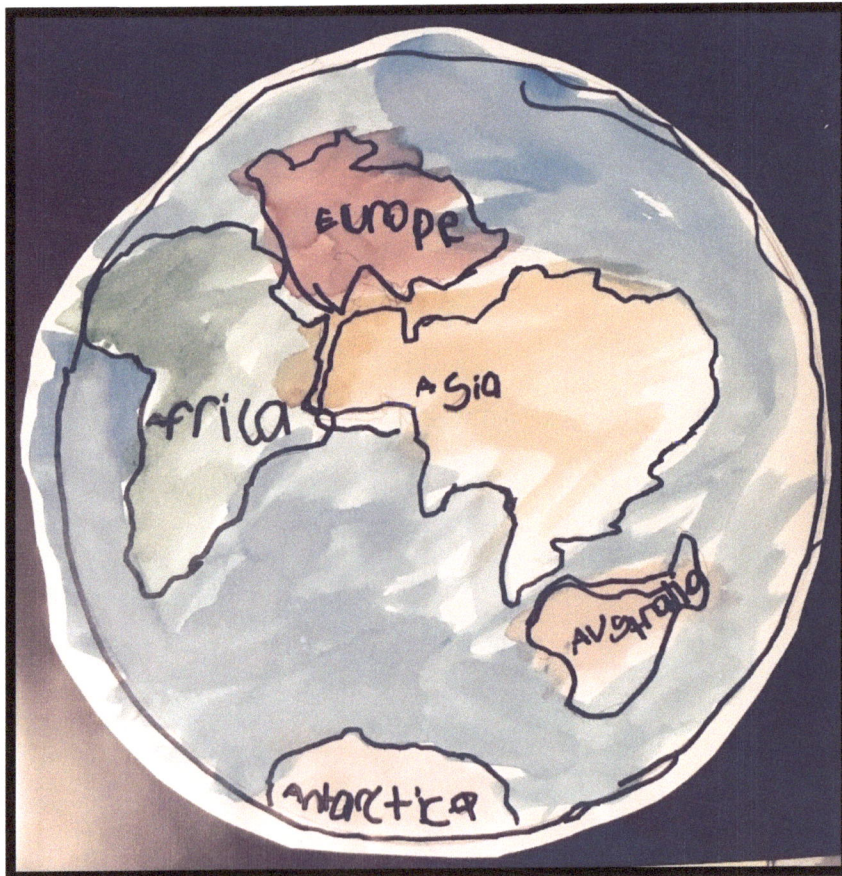

Children are engaged with multiple queries.

rooster

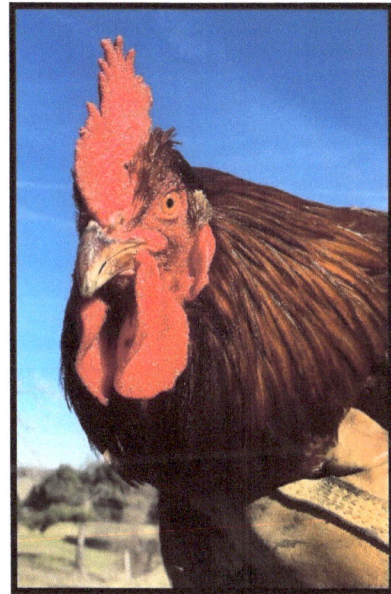

Do not do for a child what they can do on their own.

The seeds of confidence are carefully sown.

We honor uninterrupted time and an orderly place.

The mind is absorbing at each child's pace.

What is Montessori?
I hope you now know.

It is
Maria's ideas
that help
children grow!

Maria Montessori
1870-1952

www.ingramcontent.com/pod-product-compliance
Lightning Source LLC
LaVergne TN
LVHW072102070426
835508LV00002B/223